This Book belongs to

Date --------------------------------------

Presented by

*The Saints—like Peter and Mary Magdalene—
lead us to Christ.*

New...Saint Joseph

BEGINNER'S BOOK
OF SAINTS

By
Rev. Lawrence G. Lovasik, S.V.D.
Divine Word Missionary

CATHOLIC BOOK PUBLISHING CO.
New Jersey

CONTENTS

NIHIL OBSTAT: Francis J. McAree, S.T.D., Censor Librorum

IMPRIMATUR: ✝ Patrick J. Sheridan, D.D., Vicar General, Archdiocese of New York

The Nihil Obstat and Imprimatur are official declarations that a book or pamphlet is free of doctrinal or moral error. No implication is contained therein that those who have granted the Nihil Obstat and Imprimatur agree with the contents, opinions, or statements expressed.

INTRODUCTION

Saints are persons who have lived very holy Christian lives on earth and are now in heaven. The Church offers them as models for us to imitate.

The Church says: "Here are some models for you to follow. If you do what the Saints did, according to your ability, and listen to their counsel, you can achieve what they achieved."

This is one of the main reasons for the Church's custom of honoring the Saints. They are not only our intercessors in heaven but also examples of virtue for us on earth.

May this book on the lives of the Saints help you not only to know them but also to imitate their lives and seek their help before God.

MARY, MOTHER OF GOD
Queen of all Saints

Feast: January 1 — August 22   Died: 1st century A.D.

What joy there was in heaven the day Jesus called His Mother Mary home! He would not permit the devil to have any power over His Virgin Mother. So He took her to heaven with soul and body.

And then He crowned her Queen of Heaven—of Angels and Saints. She was raised above all the Saints because of her fullness of grace and the splendor of her virtues.

Now she intercedes for her children on earth. And her prayers are so powerful because Jesus is pleased to grant the requests of Mary's Immaculate Heart.

PRAYER: Dearest Mother Mary, help me in all dangers on the journey to our heavenly home.

SAINT ELIZABETH ANN SETON

Feast: January 4   *Died: 1821*

Elizabeth is known as the first American-born Saint. Born in New York City in 1774, Elizabeth Bayley was a devout Episcopalian. She married William Seton and they raised five children.

When her husband became ill, they went to Italy seeking help. But William died there. Upon returning home, Elizabeth became a Catholic.

Within a few years she opened the first parish school in America. Later she founded the Sisters of Charity, the first American teaching order of nuns, and became known as "Mother Seton."

PRAYER: Dear Mother Seton, help me to follow Jesus wherever He may lead me.

SAINT AGNES

Feast: January 21   *Died: 304*

Everywhere she went heads turned as Agnes walked by. She was very beautiful and had a friendly smile. Many young men wanted to marry her but she gave her heart to Christ.

Agnes lived in Rome many years ago when Christians were persecuted. She was only twelve years old when ordered to honor a false goddess. This would mean denying Christ, so Agnes refused.

The cruel judge had her clothes torn off before a howling mob. But Agnes remained loyal to Jesus. Then when sentenced to death, she joyfully bowed her head to the sword and went to be with Jesus forever.

PRAYER: Saint Agnes, help me to be pure and always faithful to Jesus.

SAINT JOHN BOSCO

Feast: January 31   *Died: 1888*

As a priest in Italy, John was dedicated to helping young boys and girls. He started by aiding homeless boys. Soon word spread that there was a priest who really cared.

He educated them in their faith and in the trades. When his boys left, they could go out in the world as skilled workers and model Christians.

To continue his work this holy man established communities of Priests, Brothers, and Nuns to assist young boys and girls. He knew how to reach out to the young with a minimum of rules but with lots of love and encouragement. He is known as the Apostle of Youth.

PRAYER: Dear Saint John, teach me how to reach out to my brothers and sisters in need.

SAINT MARGARET OF CORTONA

Feast: February 22   *Died: 1297*

Margaret felt rejected by her step-mother. So, while a teenager, she ran away with a young man and gave birth to a child without being married. When her partner was killed, Margaret returned to her hometown of Cortona.

For three years she did public penance for her sins. Then she joined the Franciscan Third Order and served the sick poor. Over twenty years were spent with these suffering brothers and sisters as she saw her Crucified Savior in each one.

By word and example, Margaret helped many people come back to God.

PRAYER: O Model of Penitents, help me to repent whenever I displease God.

SAINT DOMINIC SAVIO

Feast: March 9   *Died: 1857*

Not long ago in Italy Dominic eagerly prepared for First Communion. Now his special day arrived and he welcomed Jesus into his heart. What could he give in return?

He gave Jesus his spotless heart and resolved to die rather than ever sin. Then as a teenager hoping to become a priest, he was a pupil of the great Saint John Bosco. Dominic studied hard and loved to pray. But his health was poor and soon he had to return home.

He accepted his sickness. For nothing could take away his joy in loving and serving God. And Dominic was called home to heaven when only fifteen years old.

PRAYER: Dear Saint Dominic, help me to find my greatest joy in loving and serving God.

SAINT PATRICK

Feast: March 17   *Died: 461*

Did you know that Patrick once was a slave? When he was sixteen Patrick was captured by pirates, taken to Ireland, and sold as a slave.

Six years later he escaped and returned home. In a dream he was told to go back and bring the Faith to Ireland. As a priest, he labored for a time in England. Then the Pope made him a bishop and sent him to Ireland.

Despite the hostility of the Druids, Patrick planted the seeds of Faith all over Ireland. By his example, preaching, and gift of miracles, Patrick helped to change a pagan nation into a land strong in the Faith. Thus the former slave freed the Irish people.

PRAYER: Glorious Saint Patrick, help me to be always grateful for the gift of Faith.

SAINT JOSEPH

Feast: March 19   *Died: 1st century A.D.*

Joseph, a carpenter of Nazareth, was chosen by God to be the foster father of Jesus and the husband of the Blessed Virgin Mary. What an honor, privilege, and responsibility!

Things weren't always easy. Shortly after Christ's birth in Bethlehem, King Herod sought to kill the Child. So Joseph fled to Egypt with Jesus and Mary.

Returning to Nazareth, Joseph worked hard in his carpenter shop to support the Holy Family. To his loving care was entrusted the childhood and youth of the Redeemer of the world. When his labors were over, he died in the arms of Jesus and Mary.

PRAYER: Dear Guardian of the Holy Family, please watch over me and be my guardian.

SAINT CATHERINE OF SIENA

Feast: April 29   *Died: 1380*

Catherine gave her heart to God at a very early age. At eighteen she became a member of the Dominican Third Order devoted to helping the poor. Many hours were spent in prayer before the Crucifix. And in later years, Catherine bore the wounds of Christ on her body.

Catherine brought many sinners back to God. And her counsel was sought by thousands for she had one of the finest minds of her time.

Often called upon to be a peacemaker, Catherine persuaded the Pope who had been living in France to return to Rome. She wrote books about spiritual matters and has been declared a Doctor of the Church.

PRAYER: Dear Saint Catherine, teach me how to live a life of prayer and service to others.

SAINT RITA

Feast: May 22   *Died: 1457*

Rita wanted to enter a convent, but her parents arranged a marriage for her. Trusting in God, she obeyed their wishes and became a good wife and mother,

Her husband mistreated Rita, but she remained faithful to her duties. When her husband and sons died, she became an Augustinian nun.

Rita had a fervent love for the Crucified Savior. And she had a wound on her forehead as if struck by a thorn from the Crucifix. Rita calmly accepted all suffering for love of Jesus. Because her intercession has won remarkable favors from God, she is the Saint of the Impossible.

PRAYER: *Dear Saint Rita, help me to find courage and strength in the Cross of Christ.*

SAINT JOAN OF ARC

Feast: May 30   *Died: 1431*

Joan had a most unusual vocation for a teenage girl. At seventeen she was called to defend her country and the Faith. She had been helping her family on their farm and often went to the chapel to pray and receive Jesus in Holy Communion.

Going to the king, Joan asked for a small army. He believed that God had sent her to save France so he gave her a band of soldiers. Joan led them carrying her banner with the words: "Jesus, Mary." The inspired troops drove the enemy into retreat.

Later, Joan was captured by the enemy and cruelly put to death. She died crying out, "Jesus, Jesus."

PRAYER: O Teenage Soldier of God, help me to follow Jesus with your heroic courage.

SAINT ANTHONY OF PADUA

Feast: June 13   *Died: 1231*

Word spread rapidly through the town: "Father Anthony is coming!" Everyone ran to hear him—this man of God, this Wonderworker.

They loved to hear him preach about God. This day he began, "God so loved the world that He sent His only Son." Soon many were weeping tears of joy at the thought of God's great love. Others were shedding tears of sorrow that they didn't serve Him better. All knew deep in their hearts that God loved them.

Anthony is invoked by those seeking to find something that was lost. He especially helps lost sinners find their way back to God.

PRAYER: *O Saint Anthony, help me to realize how much God loves us.*

SAINT PETER THE APOSTLE

Feast: June 29   *Died: 64 A.D.*

Peter was a lovable impulsive man who always let you know where he stood. He was the first Apostle to acknowledge Christ as the Son of God. And when some followers left Jesus, Peter assured Him that the Apostles would never leave Him.

On Pentecost, helped by the Holy Spirit, Peter preached to a large crowd. Over 3000 people were baptized. This was the beginning of the Church. And Peter was the first Pope.

Some enemies of the Church tried to stop him from telling people about Jesus. Peter let them know where he stood. And in the end, he gave up his life preaching the Name of Jesus.

PRAYER: Dear Saint Peter, help me to always honor and respect the Holy Name of Jesus.

BLESSED JUNIPERO SERRA

Feast: July 1   *Died: 1784*

Many cities in California have beautiful names—Los Angeles (The Angels), San Francisco (Saint Francis). These are the names of missions founded by Father Serra.

Miguel José Serra was born in Spain. He took the name Junipero when he became a Franciscan priest. Then he was sent as a missionary to Mexico.

Later he went to the Mexican province of California (now the State of California). And he established missions all along the coast while bringing thousands of people to God. Worn out by his service to his Master, he was called home to the heavenly banquet.

PRAYER: Blessed Junipero, help me to make Jesus known and loved by all people.

BLESSED KATERI TEKAKWITHA

Feast: July 14   *Died: 1680*

Kateri was born in New York of the Mohawk tribe. From Jesuit missionaries she learned about God's love for all people and about the Savior Who died to save us.

As a teenager she became a Christian. And at her First Communion, she gave her heart to Jesus. Some members of the tribe threatened the Christians, so Kateri fled to safety in the Christian Colony in Canada.

Every morning, even in bitter cold, she attended Mass. And as soon as Jesus came into her heart in Communion, she didn't feel the cold any more. She died at the age of twenty-four.

PRAYER: Blessed Kateri, help me to prepare well to receive Jesus in Holy Communion.

SAINT ANN

Feast: July 26   *Died: 1st Century B.C.*

Ann and her husband Joachim lived in Nazareth before Christ was born. They had no children, so they prayed for a child for many years.

At last a daughter was born to Ann. She was called Miriam or "Mary." Ann taught Mary to read the Scriptures. And she offered her to God in the service of the Temple.

Years later Mary returned to Nazareth. The Archangel Gabriel appeared and told Mary that she would be the Mother of the Son of God.

Ann prayed only for a child and she became mother of the Mother of God!

PRAYER: *O Mother of the Mother of God, keep me always close to Jesus and Mary.*

SAINT MAXIMILIAN KOLBE

Feast: August 14   *Died: 1941*

Jesus said, "Greater love than this no one has than to lay down one's life for his friend." Maximilian laid down his life for another. Where did he get such love and courage?

Maximilian was a Franciscan priest in Poland who had a most fervent devotion to the Immaculate Virgin Mary. Through Mary Maximilian grew in love for her Crucified Son and tried to be more like Him.

During World War II while in a concentration camp, Maximilian offered himself in place of a condemned man. So through Mary he received the love and courage, and finally, the heavenly reward.

PRAYER: Dear Saint Maximilian, help me to imitate your love for our Blessed Mother Mary.

SAINT ROSE OF LIMA

Feast: August 23   *Died: 1617*

"Mother, only beauty of the soul is important," Rose answered when asked to wear beautiful clothes. Even as a child she wanted only to please God.

Rose was born in Lima, Peru, in 1586. To help her poor parents, she grew flowers and made blankets. Refusing offers of marriage, Rose became a Dominican Tertiary living a life of prayer and penance at home.

When her parents died, Rose spent the rest of her life caring for the sick and most needy.

Soon after Rose was called to her heavenly reward, she was declared the first Saint of the Americas.

PRAYER: Dear Saint Rose, obtain for me the grace to know what is important in life.

SAINT AUGUSTINE OF HIPPO

Feast: August 28   *Died: 430*

Augustine was Bishop of Hippo in North Africa. The early Church was threatened by many false teachings. With his keen mind he showed the people how to recognize the true teachings of Christ. And his sermons inspired them to cling to the true Faith.

As a youth Augustine sought earthly pleasures. But the prayers of his mother, Saint Monica, helped to bring about his conversion.

He wrote many volumes about the spiritual life that have been read throughout the ages. Augustine is renowned as a Doctor of the Church who taught Christians how to thirst after God alone.

PRAYER: *Dear Saint Augustine, teach me how to seek God alone.*

SAINT VINCENT DE PAUL

Feast: September 27   *Died: 1660*

Vincent could never pass by a beggar or a homeless person without trying to help. As a priest in France, he gathered people around him to serve the poor. The men collected food and clothing and the women cooked and assisted the sick.

To continue his work Vincent started religious communities of men and women dedicated to serving the poor with his spirit of charity. He built homes for the poor, the sick, the aged, and abandoned children.

He spent himself every day striving to relieve suffering. Yet in spite of many distractions, his soul was always close to God through prayer.

PRAYER: Dear Apostle of Charity, help me to imitate your kindness to the poor.

SAINT THERESA OF THE CHILD JESUS

Feast: October 1   *Died: 1897*

Theresa wanted to save souls by prayer and sacrifice. So she entered a Carmelite convent in France when she was only fifteen years old.

Her Little Way consisted in doing ordinary things each day, as perfectly as possible and with as much love as possible, to please God. It meant child-like love of God our Father with complete trust and self-surrender.

Before long Theresa contracted tuberculosis. When she was near death, she said she would spend her heaven "teaching souls my Little Way of trust and self-surrender."

PRAYER: *Dear Saint Theresa, help me to offer little things to God each day with love.*

SAINT FRANCIS OF ASSISI

Feast: October 4   *Died: 1226*

It all seemed so simple to Francis. Since the same God created all mankind and all creatures, he would love all people and *all creatures* as his brothers and sisters.

Francis lived in Italy at a time when people's hearts had grown cold. God called him to show them how to live as true Christians.

So Francis went about calling people to amend their lives. Soon others joined him and the Franciscan Order was started. Their message of joy for the love of Christ shown in the Cross moved thousands to repentance. The love that was missing in many hearts was rekindled.

PRAYER: *Dear Saint Francis, help me to find joy in loving and serving God.*

SAINT TERESA OF JESUS

Feast: October 15   *Died: 1582*

God loves a cheerful giver. Teresa was a Carmelite in Spain at a time when some religious didn't serve God generously. So God chose Teresa to stir up their hearts.

Teresa taught the nuns in her own convent to return to the ways of solitude, fasting, and prayer. Then she traveled through Spain founding new convents and improving others. And she suffered greatly from those who opposed her.

Teresa gave of herself wholeheartedly in serving God and helping others. She wrote books about the spiritual life and she is a Doctor of the Church.

PRAYER: *O Saint Teresa, teach me how to serve God with a generous heart.*

SAINT MARTIN DE PORRES

Feast: November 3   *Died: 1639*

Born in Peru in 1579, Martin grew up in poverty and had a deep love for the poor and all creatures.

As a Dominican brother, Martin performed the most humble tasks with joy for love of God. His nights were spent in prayer and penance. Martin's days were filled nursing the sick and helping those in need of food or a word of encouragement.

The Saint even found time to run a hospital for animals.

God was pleased with Martin's works and blessed him with the gift of healing. When the Archbishop of Mexico was very sick, Martin cured him with the touch of his hand.

PRAYER: O Saint Martin, teach me to help my neighbor for love of God.

SAINT FRANCIS XAVIER

Feast: December 3   *Died: 1552*

Francis was a powerful preacher blessed with the gift to touch souls. A Spaniard by birth, Francis helped Saint Ignatius form the Society of Jesus. And he vowed to work for the conversion of souls.

After he became a priest, Francis set sail for India. In a short time as a result of his sermons and example, many people were converted to Christ.

Then Francis carried the light of Faith to Japan. Here too, a flourishing Christian community soon arose. Francis had a deep love for the Blessed Virgin Mary. Many unbelievers were won over through her intercession.

PRAYER: *Saint Francis Xavier, help me to offer prayers each day to bring souls to Christ.*

PRAYER TO
MY PATRON SAINT

Dear Saint, N.,
I bear your name,
which you have made famous
by your holiness.

Obtain God's grace for me
that I may grow in goodness.

Grant that by imitating you
I may imitate our Lord Jesus.

Watch over me all my life
and bring me safe to my heavenly
home.